Peter Oswald

THE RAMAYANA

a play of the Hindu Epic

T0262452

OBERON BOOKS
LONDON

WWW.OBERONBOOKS.COM

First published in 2000 by Oberon Books Ltd
521 Caledonian Road, London N7 9RH
Tel: +44 (0) 20 7607 3637 / Fax: +44 (0) 20 7607 3629
e-mail: info@oberonbooks.com
www.oberonbooks.com

A catalogue record for this book is available from the British Library.

PB ISBN: 978-1-84002-201-8

Visit www.oberonbooks.com to read more about all our books
and to buy them. You will also find features, author interviews and
news of any author events, and you can sign up for e-newsletters
so that you're always first to hear about our new releases.

Characters

PROLOGUE

RAMA, prince of Ayodhya

SITA, his princess

LAKSHMAN, his brother

BHARATHA, his father

RAVANA, the demon King of Lanka

SOORPANAKHA, his sister

MARICHA, his uncle

MANDODARI, his wife

INDRAJIT, his son

VIBISHANA, his brother

MAHARSHWA, his commander

SUGRIVA, the King of the monkeys

TARA, his wife

HANUMAN

NILA

JAMBAVAN, King of the Bears

SAMPATI, an eagle

JATAYU, his brother

VARUNA, the god of the sea

BEARS, MONKEYS, DEMONS

DEMON WITCHES

The Ramayana was first performed at the Birmingham Rep Theatre on 20th October 2000, with the following cast:

PROLOGUE, Saul Jaffe, Thushani Weerasekera/
    Jimmy Akingbola

RAMA, Gerald Kyd

SITA, Ayesha Dharker

LAKSHMAN, Paul Sharma

BHARATHA, Guy Rhys

RAVANA, Andrew French

SOORPANAKHA, Charlotte Bicknell

MARICHA, Saul Jaffe

MANDODARI, Inika Leigh-Wright

INDRAJIT, Arif Javid

VIBISHANA, Enoch Frost

MAHARSHWA, Jimmy Akingbola

SUGRIVA, Vincent Ebrahim

TARA, Thushani Weerasekera

HANUMAN, Miltos Yerolemou

NILA, Danny Scheinmann

JAMBAVAN, George Eggay

SAMPATI, Eugene Salleh

JATAYU, Eugene Salleh

VARUNA, Company

BEARS, MONKEYS, DEMONS, Company

DEMON WITCHES, Pooja Kumar/ Thushani Weeraseker

Director, Indhu Rubasingham

Designer, Ultz

Choreographer, Piali Ray

Composer, Kuljit Bhamra

The play takes place in Ayodhya, in the Dandaka forest, by the sea and inside and outside the city of Lanka.

PROLOGUE

Enter the full company.

PROLOGUE: Shall I tell you something frightening? There is a demon. His name is Ravana. He has ten heads. He is the King of the demons and they fly through the world and whenever they find someone praying they kill them! Do you think this isn't true? Have you seen many people praying recently? No one dares! And you may say, if God is God, why doesn't he destroy the demon? I will tell you! A long time ago the demon knelt down with his two brothers on a mountain and he prayed for a thousand years! A very religious demon! And when the thousand years came to an end, the demon was so holy that God had to give him whatever he wanted! So he asked that he should never be able to be killed by any god or any other demon! Now nothing in heaven or hell can hurt him! He has all power over everyone on earth and people live only to die, they have forgotten heaven! People go mad by the time they are fourteen, they murder each other just to pass the time, because the parents have no answers to the questions of their children. They have let go – the world has let go – oh – let go of heaven! But I will dare to pray, I would rather die than go mad, I will dare to cry out, God help me! God help me! Come down!

He hears an answer to his prayer.

What's that? What's that? What are you saying? If God came down as a human being – as a human being he could kill the demon! Ravana did not ask for protection against mere humans – but if God was a human! Or if humans were God – goodbye demon! And it has happened! God has come down to earth. But now God has been born with a special force and extra presence in four brothers and one woman – Sita, a princess. And the oldest of the brothers is Rama. Sita and Rama have found each other and they have been married. But this King, Rama's father, has been tricked into banishing him for fourteen years to the forest – and Sita has gone with him and so has his brother Lackshman. Rama was about to be crowned regent, but now the old king, because of the trick, must crown another of the brothers, Bharata. But these brothers love each other – they would never take anything from each other. They are God in human form. They have come to conquer the demon. Oh Rama! How will you fight the demon in rags in the place of tigers? But already I can pray more easily. I will trust in you! I will watch what you do!

End of Prologue.

SCENE 1

The forest. RAMA in prayer with SITA. Animals move about and birds sing.

LAKSHMAN: Brother, our country's army is approaching!
Cavalry, elephants and infantry –
They must have hacked a broad road through the jungle,
To get to us! Our brother Bharatha
Is coming to destroy us and secure
The throne his mother stole for him! Oh Rama!

RAMA: Do not suspect him of such madness, Lakshman!

Enter BHARATHA, who throws himself at RAMA's feet.

BHARATHA: Rama!

RAMA goes to him and raises him up.

RAMA: Brother, I see that something bad has happened,
Worse than my exile, that has brought you here,
Carrying such a brimful jar of tears
To pour out at my feet. But has that brought you
So little comfort that you cannot speak?

BHARATHA: Rama!

SITA: Your road was very long and on the way
You have stored up as many words as tears;
The tears are over, now the words must flow.

RAMA: My ears are open!

BHARATHA: All the blame is mine!

RAMA: For what, sweet Bharatha?

BHARATHA: The King our father
        Has left this life!

RAMA: What took him from his body?

BHARATHA: The lack of you! The cunning of my mother!

SITA: Now let the ball of agony unravel.

BHARATHA: It was for me that she desired your exile,
    And dragged it from him with such force she killed him –
    So losing us his light and yours for nothing,
    Since how could I ascend a lion's throne
    Without the laughter of the world destroying
    The littleness I am? Oh teach me, brother!
    Now I have no road open but to cry
    To you for help, to beg you to return!

RAMA: We must obey our father's last command
    As if it were the law that fixed the stars,
    You must secure the safety of Ayodhya
    For fourteen years, that is your only duty.
    I ask you then what you are doing here.

BHARATHA: We cannot live without you in Ayodhya!

RAMA: Our father died to keep the word he gave.
    How can we disobey him, or break faith
    With any man no longer in the body?

BHARATHA: Oh do not make me reign where you should reign!

SITA: Bharatha, you will never be forgotten!
    The place you earn will be a sacred one!
    The memory of how you served will be
    A healing river in this world forever.

RAMA: You must return, but we will not be parted.
    I shall go barefoot.

    He takes off his sandals and gives them to BHARATHA.

BHARATHA: Sweet teacher, you have given me a way
    To reign beneath you, since I have to reign.
    Rama, I shall not sit upon your throne,
    But place these sandals on that seat of judgement,
    And take my place beneath them, as a sign
    That at the height of power I am lower
    That what you walk on! I am not a King,

I am the dust beneath the feet of Rama!

They embrace.

I count the days. I cannot rule Ayodhya
One minute longer than the fourteen years
Our father said!

RAMA: We shall obey precisely!

Exeunt.

SCENE 2

A curtain rises and falls – on the curtain is written, 'ten years pass'. SITA and RAMA in the forest.

SITA: My husband, are you dreaming of the city?

RAMA: The people of the city are all here.
See how these saplings bending in the wind
Are children doing up their shoes –

SITA: Schoolchildren –
But fallen leaves are bare feet scampering
Between tall tree-legs –

RAMA: Birds are late for weddings
Of which they are themselves the decorations,
They race from branch to branch down streets of air,
Screaming with laughter!

RAMA senses a demon approaching.

Violence comes this way, announced by silence!

SITA: I had forgotten all about the demons!

Exit.

RAMA: Fighting to hide the terror it contains,
It sweats within, it stores up hate like steam.
What will it be, a tiger with two horns,
A giant reaching out with five-mile arms?
No – look – and see – another kind of demon!

Enter SOORPANAKHA dancing. She stops, stunned by the sight of RAMA, and falls at his feet.

8

SOORPANAKHA: Oh save me from myself!

RAMA: Yourself, my lady?

SOORPANAKHA: I must have love or I will burst into flames,
    Birth a fireball that'll roll through these trees!
    You be an iron mountain, I'll be the thunderstorm
    Kissing and kissing your peak with lightning!

RAMA: What brought you?

SOORPANAKHA: Ask no questions, here I am,
    I am seed scattered, grow where I'm sown,
    Oh dig me in and press me down,
    Before the mad breeze wanders me on!

RAMA: What are you asking?

SOORPANAKHA: Marry me! Cry to me – You are mine, you are
    mine!
    Make something of me! Look, I am sand,
    I am an opinion – help me I'm changing
                            I am collapsible – oh make me stand!

RAMA: I cannot be your husband. I am married,
    And I have sworn to love one wife alone.

SOORPANAKHA: I hope that she will not die soon!

RAMA: I have a brother who is just like me.
    And he is married, but he has not seen
    His wife for ten years. Have a look at him.
    Lakshman!

    Enter LAKSHMAN.

LAKSHMAN: Oh Rama! Am I in a dream?
    Who is this woman?

RAMA: By a miracle
    This beauty found us in the wilderness
    And by another she desires one thing –
    To be your wife.

SOORPANAKHA: My life begins.
    This is a new sky – too bright! Two suns!

LAKSHMAN: But you will not be satisfied with me!

9

My elder brother is a thing of wonder;
I am his slave, and if you marry me,
You'll be the better half of less than nothing.
Marry this man and make yourself my mistress.

SOORPANAKHA: *(To RAMA.)* Brother says to marry me.

RAMA: I am besotted with monogamy!
He is my slave, however, as he says,
I am his master and I will command him.
Marry her!

LAKSHMAN: Could you love me properly?
You loved him first!

SOORPANAKHA: *(To RAMA.)* I loved you first.

RAMA: Then you must swear to love him more than me.

SOORPANAKHA: *(To LAKSHMAN.)*
It was not love. I hate him now.
He was a prophecy of you.

LAKSHMAN: My love is at the end of hesitation –
But wait! Dear God! How could I have forgotten?
My wife! My wife!

RAMA: He still remembers her.
Oh dear, I thought that he would not have done.

SOORPANAKHA: You are my love! The prophecy was wrong!
Love me!

RAMA: How can I when my wife is living?

She goes to LAKSHMAN.

LAKSHMAN: And I am married to my memory!

SOORPANAKHA: *(Explodes, revealing her demon nature.)*
Not much to chose between love and hunger!
Beware!
Love-starved I'll stuff my face with what I've longed for!

LAKSHMAN: What can I say? My wife is in the city.

RAMA: My wife is here.

Enter SITA.

SOORPANAKHA: Little cloud of separation;
    Wall of petals that's my prison;
    Half-imagine how I want him
    And your blood will burst your veins!

RAMA: This demon woman wants to marry me.
    Would you agree?

SITA: My love, I set you free.

RAMA: Then I choose freely not to go to her.

LAKSHMAN: I must be loyal to my wife, forgive me.

SOORPANAKHA: I will reduce your choice!

She goes to attack SITA. LAKSHMAN grabs her and at a sign from RAMA does not kill her but cuts off her breasts.

                        My Beauty!
    I came to you for love! You are not human!

RAMA: It is a sign, a challenge and a warning.

SOORPANAKHA: I am the sister of the King,
    Ravana! Now you see what you have done!
    You will not sleep from this day on,
    You will be waiting to be murdered!
    Has the sky changed? It is your mother –
    Into your grave she peers and pours.

RAMA: Go to your brother. Say you come from Rama.
    Your bleeding breasts shall be my messengers.

SITA: So – war.

RAMA: It was for this we were born.

Exeunt all but SOORPANAKHA.

SCENE 3

The court of RAVANA in Lanka. MAHAPARSHWA, INDRAJIT, MANDODARI, DEMONS. SOORPANAKHA on the ground.

RAVANA: Were you asleep?

SOORPANAKHA: No I was not asleep –

RAVANA: You were outnumbered! How many?

SOORPANAKHA: Two of them!

RAVANA: Two!

SOORPANAKHA: I fell in love with them!

RAVANA: In love with humans?

SOORPANAKHA: They are not like humans!
   As rain to earth when earth is cracking
   I came to them, they came to me,
   So I believed, so I believed!

RAVANA: What does this sign mean? What is this word of war?
   How can a human dare? Indrajit, my son, even greater than I
   am, what can you say to me?

INDRAJIT: Shall we fight a human?

MAHAPARSHWA: How does this fit into our scheme of things?

RAVANA: He kills my demons – that I could ignore.
   He makes my sister ugly – that I cannot ignore.

MANDODARI: Rama is God come down in human form!
   You must not fight him! That would be your end!

Demons burst out all at once.

MAHAPARSHWA: How does this fit?

MANDODARI: You shall not fight!

INDRAJIT: Your grave, Mother!

SOORPANAKHA: My beauty!

VIBISHANA: Rama is God!

RAVANA: Mandodari, my first wife, I keep you by me for a
   purpose: whatever you say, I do the opposite. So God comes
   down. Would it be polite to ignore him?

INDRAJIT: God says, what is the one thing I cannot have? Death.
   Who will give it to me? Ravana, demon King of Lanka.

RAVANA: Sorcerer, you see far!

MANDODARI: Right to the bottom of the pit!

INDRAJIT: Your grave, Mother!

VIBISHANA: Brother, when you and I, to gain great power,
Prayed on the mountain for a thousand years,
Great God was forced by our restraint to grant us
Whatever we desired. Because I love him,
I asked him for a heart of adoration;
You asked the Lord to bless you with protection
From all the gods.

RAVANA: And so their end began!

VIBISHANA: But in your pride you asked for no protection
Against mankind! And so you must consider:
A god could kill you if he was a man.

RAVANA: If God is a human he can kill me. If God is a human I
can kill him.

SOORPANAKHA: You must not kill him!

RAVANA: What shall we do to him?

SOORPANAKHA: Brother, death is less than nothing!
He lives for someone else. He keeps beside him
A woman like a winter dawn
Whose eyes see straight through death to heaven;
Where she walks the sky falls open
And she stands blazing like a starflower
Rooted in nothing. She was made for you.
Her name is Sita. Heaven dreams of her.
Rama will be far worse than dead without her!

RAVANA: She could end the world, this woman. I will capture
her!

MANDODARI: I have to speak! It is my sacred duty!
There is no crime on earth, in hell or heaven,
More vile than this: to part a wife and husband!
Even to dream it is to die within.

RAVANA: But we are demons! Why has God come down
If not to fight us? Our abominations
Rising, have pierced the silence of his heaven
At last! And should we therefore turn to lambs,

Running behind him? Sita like a star
Fallen to earth is mine to take – and more –
I say she is the universe transformed
Into a woman to be lost and won!
The darkness shall be brighter than the light.

MARICHA: *(In terror.)* Rama! Rama! Rama! Rama!

RAVANA: And you will be my trap, Maricha!

MARICHA: He is here! He is here!

RAVANA: Maricha, uncle, you once fought Rama! Great warrior, teacher, excellent shape-shifter, you are to be my help in this last adventure! Turn into a golden deer!

MAHAPARSHWA: How does this?

MARICHA turns into a golden deer and runs about. The others laugh and scream with delight.

SOORPANAKHA: Oh Rama, Rama! Catch me that golden deer!

RAVANA: I will do so, Sita! And now I leave her side!
Maricha, cry out in Rama's voice!

MARICHA: Oh Sita! Lakshman! Help me!

MAHAPARSHWA as LAKSHMAN leaves SOORPANAKHA's side.

SOORPANAKHA: Go, Lakshman, save him!

RAVANA: Now she is alone!

MANDODARI: Sita is also God.

MARICHA: Ravana, kill me, kill me!

RAVANA: Maricha, you taught me warfare, you fought Rama, and you still breathe air!

MARICHA: No more, no more, no more!

RAVANA: I desire her!

Exeunt.

SCENE 4

The jungle. Enter RAMA and SITA to a fire.

SITA: The moment has arrived.

RAMA: Now Ravana
    Has felt your glory. He cannot be killed
    By any other human hand –
    We must cast off divinity, descend
    Into the dream, complete what we began
    By being born.

SITA: Then God is man and woman.

RAMA: Until this moment, all that we have suffered
    We have not suffered – we have entered exile
    Smiling, and lost my father with no tears,
    Because we see at all times all of time;
    But now the time has come for us to change.

SITA: And by a story acted out in life,
    Reveal the truth, how that this life on earth
    Is heaven-bent, except that demon tricks
    Cloud the heart's eyes with dreams of greed and hate.

RAMA: Our life will be a light that casts no shadows.
    Ravana must be tempted by your beauty,
    To cause his own fall, and humanity
    Will tell that story till the end of stories.

SITA: If I am to permit indignity,
    I must cast off my power, that is fire,
    Into the fire. I will depend on you
    To come for me – and you will come for me –

RAMA: Then you will take back from the guardian fire,
    Your radiance!

SITA casts off her divinity into the fire.

SITA: Heaven farewell. Now Sita is alone.

They embrace fearfully.

RAMA: Why are you frightened? We have come from heaven –
    Remember!

SITA: I remember. I will say
    That mantra every minute of the day,
    Sita, remember you have come from heaven!
    I will remember when I saw your face
    For the first time, when your bright chariot
    Passed by the window of my father's palace,
    And you looked up, and I remembered heaven.
    But it is so dark!

RAMA: Now the play begins!
    Now God performs the passions of a man!

SITA: Lakshman is coming!

RAMA: He must not be told
    What we have done. We must depend on him
    To fight for us in faith whatever happens.

    Enter LAKSHMAN with fruit.

LAKSHMAN: Fruit!

    SITA falls on the fruit greedily. LAKSHMAN senses danger.

    Into the hut – a demon is approaching.

RAMA: Listen to Lakshman – he is your protection.

SITA: How can he help me?

RAMA: What could strike down Lakshman?
    This man of absolute religion –

SITA: Lakshman, look up!

LAKSHMAN: Please, goddess, I have sworn
    That I will never look into your eyes
    While you are dwelling in a woman's body!

SITA: How am I safe when he is guarding me?
    What if a spider dropped into my hair?

RAMA: It would not dare.

SITA: He would just stand there saying,
    Nothing has happened to her ankles. Lakshman!

LAKSHMAN: I am beside you!

SITA: Help! A demon bee

Is in my hair!

LAKSHMAN: Extract it with your fingers!
Demon, reveal yourself and fight with Lakshman!

RAMA: Lakshman, the bees are in her brain today.
Sita, you see how well he would defend you!

SITA: I see how loudly he would stamp and threaten.

LAKSHMAN: That is the language demons understand!

SITA: Thanks be to Lakshman! Under his protection,
Nothing can happen to my toes and shins!

Enter a golden deer frolicking.

Look at that golden deer! The sun transformed!
The moon with four legs! Catch it for me Rama!

LAKSHMAN: If I may ask this question, holy mother,
Why are you glad about a golden deer?
Bright things have never drawn your eyes before!
As for myself – I fear it is a demon!

SITA: Blasphemy! Beauty is the child of God!

LAKSHMAN: Yes, and temptation is a demon's daughter.

SITA: What is this creature tempting me to do?
Stroke it? Oh Lakshman, is that such a sin?

LAKSHMAN: It wants to lead your lord away from you.

SITA: But there would still be you. I ask you, Rama,
Is it a demon?

RAMA: If you want it, Sita,
With all your heart, then I will catch it for you.

LAKSHMAN: No, you must leave it! Listen to me, Rama!

SITA: Lakshman has demons on the mind, poor thing!
Am I a demon, Lakshman? Is your brother?
Lakshman, be careful of the demon flowers!

LAKSHMAN: A golden deer? That is an evil creature!

SITA: It shies away!

RAMA: It shall be yours.

LAKSHMAN: Disaster!

RAMA chases the deer. Exit deer pursued by RAMA.

Now they leap out on us from everywhere!
But I will stab and hack before I die!

SITA: Nothing.

LAKSHMAN: This glade is open on all sides.
We must fall back into the hut.

SITA: Alright.

Exeunt.

RAMA: *(Voice off.)* Oh Sita! Lakshman! Help me!

Re-enter LAKSHMAN and SITA.

SITA: Are you a demon? Run and save your brother!

LAKSHMAN: He said to stay here.

SITA: He cried out, Sita, Lakshman!

LAKSHMAN: Unlikely.

SITA: We heard him!

LAKSHMAN: A demon copied his voice.

SITA: Rama is dying!

LAKSHMAN: Rama left me in command. And I decide that what
we heard cannot have been him!

SITA: Oh, now I see – oh –

LAKSHMAN: That is my decision.

SITA: Oh, now I see inside you, Lakshman – ah horrible! Worse
than any demon, the difference between the out and the in –

LAKSHMAN: What do you mean?

SITA: Ha! How could I have believed?

LAKSHMAN: What you see is what I am.

SITA: Waiting for this chance, as patient as death – now demons
are hacking him to pieces and your heart sings!

LAKSHMAN: I would not leave him if the universe, axe in hand
was against him!

SITA: I am peering through hell's keyhole – and I see – a younger
brother! You want him dead so you can get me!

LAKSHMAN: This is a demon! Where is Sita?

SITA: Lakshman, look me in the eye and tell me you do not want
me, that you have never thought of me too warmly, anything
other than brotherly -

LAKSHMAN: God help me!

SITA: He can't do it! Oh now I understand too much. Rama could
not bring himself to tell me what he knew about you! You
have made him want to die!

LAKSHMAN: How could I desire you? I have never seen you!

SITA: What you see you can resist – but not what you imagine!
Then there is my voice, and rumours of my beauty – my
shadow falling across your face –

LAKSHMAN: I cannot hear! You cannot say this!

SITA: Then I will die with Rama!

She makes to leave.

LAKSHMAN: No! Only here is safe. Stay inside this sacred square
I will draw. It will keep you safe from all harm till I return
with Rama!

Exit having drawn square.

SITA: It is so easy to be merely human.
Oh Rama, now my story is beginning!

She jumps inside the square. Enter RAVANA disguised as a Brahmin.

RAVANA: More beautiful than fire! Must have, must hold!
Burn, burn, never learn!
(Aloud.) Ah Shiva, Vishnu, Brahma!
This is a sacred place! The atmosphere
Is pure devotion! I will kneel me down,
A humble Brahmin on his way to heaven,
And pray for years. Oh lady, give me alms!

SITA: Of course, but I must keep inside this square.

RAVANA: I am a Brahmin, I am not a demon!
    Sit down, sit down, I will recite for you,
    The entire Vedas. This will take some days –

SITA: No need, no need! I see that you are holy!

RAVANA: My dear, I cannot enter any building,
    That is my vow.

SITA: Then I will pass it over.

RAVANA: I cannot reach – my arms are weak from fasting –
    Stretch out a little further with your fingers.

He grabs her hand as she passes over the water.

Now you are mine!

SITA: Ah save me! Rama, Lakshman!

RAVANA: I hold you responsible for my loss of self-control. Oh
    help me! Stop me! Help me! Stop me!

GRASS: The path to God is closed and dead,
    The road to heaven is untrod,
    And overgrown with weeds of wrong;
    Each goes his own sweet way to ruin.

Exeunt.

SCENE 5

The same place. Enter RAMA and LAKSHMAN.

RAMA: Sita! The golden deer was an illusion!
    Lakshman was right! Because I could not catch it,
    I used my bow – it turned into a demon
    As it was dying, and it cried my name.
    Sita!

LAKSHMAN: Not here!

RAMA: She must be by the river.

LAKSHMAN: But she is not – oh God – no sign of her!

RAMA: How could you leave her?

LAKSHMAN: Oh forgive me, brother!
Sita is gone! Put all the blame on Lakshman!
But she attacked me so outrageously!

RAMA: Where is my mother? Weeping in Ayodhya
Over the horror that destroyed our father!
Our exile killed him! She has lost her son
For fourteen years! And when she hears that Sita
Has vanished, that will be another mountain
Heaped on her head! How blessed to be the mother
Of Rama!

LAKSHMAN: We must search the world for Sita!

RAMA: What watchful warriors we are! One woman
To keep between us and we choose to leave her!

LAKSHMAN: It was my fault.

RAMA: There is no worse or better –
We are just nothing and his younger brother!

LAKSHMAN: I have not seen you rage like this before!

RAMA: The world has changed into a storm of questions.
Who took her, Lakshman?

LAKSHMAN: Who on earth would dare?
How can we find her?

RAMA: When the one who hides her
Hides his own name as deep?

Enter the eagle JATAYU, whose wings have been cut off, falling to the ground with a cry.

JATAYU: Rama!

LAKSHMAN: It is our father's friend Jatayu!
Who wounded you?

JATAYU: I heard a woman screaming –
I flew to look, and it was Sita, lifted
Into the air!

RAMA strokes the eagle and soothes him.

LAKSHMAN: Jatayu, say who took her!

JATAYU: I tried to fight. He was a skyborne lion.
His chariot, drawn by mules with heads of goblins,
Winged like myself, turned swifter than a hawk.
Rama, it was the demon Ravana –

He dies.

RAMA: So now you rise to join your friend our father.
And you have blessed us with a word to guide us,
A name to say, an enemy to find!
But first we must do honour to Jatayu
Who died for us.

They kneel and pray, chant, rise and exeunt.

SCENE 6

RAVANA's court. Enter RAVANA and court with SITA.

RAVANA: Now, demons, you may feast your eyes on Sita,
Whom I have captured from our enemy,
So crushing him without a single blow –
She is the heart of God and she is mine!

INDRAJIT: Oh let me touch her!

MAHAPARSHWA: Let me kiss her!

MANDODARI: You must not touch her! She is fire!

INDRAJIT: No, she is an orange! I want to eat her!

MANDODARI: You must not eat her!

INDRAJIT: If the whole world was her that would not be enough!

MANDODARI: She is the mother of the world!

RAVANA: Sorcerer, honour your new mother!

INDRAJIT: Mother! Mother! Mother! Mother!

MAHAPARSHWA: Let me die for her!

INDRAJIT: No son has ever loved his mother like this!

MAHAPARSHWA: Let me die for her!

He starts to strangle himself.

INDRAJIT: I'll make another Sita with my spells and marry her!

SOORPANAKHA: How your beauty will change colour,
　　Tooth mark white and bruise brown purple,
　　Eyelids brushed with coal and swollen
　　With the love of Ravana!
　　You'll forget the heat of Rama
　　When you feel his spear of fire
　　And his flame tongue and his flame fingers!

MANDODARI: You must not touch her!

INDRAJIT: What plinth do you speak from? I depose you,
　　mother, make room! I want to be born again out of this
　　mother's womb!

MAHAPARSHWA: Kiss her!

RAVANA: My greatest and most easy victory –
　　The universe, my wife, to keep and change.

DEMONS: Take her! Take her now!

RAVANA: I shall not touch her. When I fly like light
　　Into the fight, worlds fall in love with me,
　　Before I crush them. Am I so deprived
　　Of love that I must take what will be given?

The DEMONS wait for SITA to come to RAVANA. She does not.

VIBISHANA: She does not want him!

MANDODARI: 　　　　　　　　Sita, you are mighty!

MAHAPARSHWA: Kill me!

SITA: Demons! You must surrender me to Rama!
　　I offer you this choice! You have gone far
　　Down the dark road, but you can still return!

RAVANA: Summon the army! March it around the city! We will
　　parade all day!

SOORPANAKHA: First her breasts –

MANDODARI: She is God! She is God!

23

RAVANA: No. This is not the way. Rama will be coming soon. Shut her in the Ashoka garden. Choose the best women you can find to persuade her.

VIBISHANA: She is God! She is God!

SITA: Now till the day he comes to set me free
With his right arm, my husband's name will be
The only word that you will get from me.

MAHAPARSHWA: Kill me! Kill me!

RAVANA: My love will change her.

Exeunt.

SCENE 7

The Chitrakuta mountain. Enter SUGRIVA, JAMBAVAN, HANUMAN, NILA, and other BEARS and MONKEYS in panic, running away from RAMA and LAKSHMAN.

SUGRIVA: Run!

JAMBAVAN: From what?

SUGRIVA: From the giants!

JAMBAVAN: Pretty tiny giants.

SUGRIVA: Escape from the enormous men!

JAMBAVAN: Stand your ground!

HANUMAN: They look lost.

JAMBAVAN: Or like they're looking for something lost.

SUGRIVA: We are lost! They are looking for us!

NILA: My lord – I have a better plan! No need to run away!

SUGRIVA: What can we do then, Nila?

NILA: Sit here and wait to die. That way we can save our energy.

SUGRIVA: Heap up a big fire, I will escape into the flames!

HANUMAN: They look so kind.

NILA: But they are humans!

JAMBAVAN: One of them is crying!

SUGRIVA: Has he heard how sad I am?

HANUMAN: Let me go down to them!

SUGRIVA: Hanuman, I need you! Don't be drawn down!
You are so soft-hearted! Some of you tough monkeys and
bears, tell him! Hold him!

HANUMAN: They are gods, they are not men!

SUGRIVA: Go on then, leave me!

NILA: My lord, why struggle? We're finished! Let him go down.

JAMBAVAN: We must at least speak to them and find out why
they have come.

SUGRIVA: Death will explain.

JAMBAVAN: We must find out!

SUGRIVA: All of you go down! I will stand here and watch you
strangled one by one. Then I will climb a tall tree and hang
myself from a vine.

JAMBAVAN: Go, Hanuman! Hide, everyone! Watch him. See
what happens!

Exeunt.

SCENE 8

Enter LAKSHMAN and RAMA, LAKSHMAN crying.

LAKSHMAN: So many countries, in the countries, caves,
In the caves, tunnels, in the tunnels, loopholes –
The demon keeps on flying through my mind,
Carrying Sita crying through the air –

Enter HANUMAN disguised as Brahmin.

Rama, a Brahmin stepping from the trees.

HANUMAN: *(Aside.)* I have disguised myself with wit and
cunning
As an unhoused and harmless holy man,
Someone to trust.

RAMA: It is a monkey, Lakshman,
    Wrapped in a cloak but we must humour him.
    Holy man, greetings!

HANUMAN: Objects of devotion,
    Wandering gods – what brings you to this jungle?
    Lords of the earth, what are you looking for?

LAKSHMAN: Monkeys.

HANUMAN: Amazing! There are millions of them!
    Why were you crying?

LAKSHMAN: We have lost a treasure.

HANUMAN: Monkeys could find it –

RAMA: Would they take us to it?

HANUMAN: Certainly! Monkeys are the best at looking,
    The best at finding and the best at taking;
    Give them a cause and they will fight like tigers –
    Otherwise they will tend to chew their fingers
    And pick fleas off the backs of one another;
    They hold down half a human conversation,
    Then they run screaming up a tree like this one,
    For no good reason, which ruins everything –
    They build no walls, no temples and no towers;
    Civilisations they have left behind them
    Not one – just nutshells and the skins of mangoes –
    But they are fiercely proud of their tradition
    Of doing nothing. But what are we doing
    Discussing monkeys? We should speak of Shiva,
    Recite the sutras and debate the Vedas.
    Are we not men of God?

LAKSHMAN: I doubt these monkeys
    Could help us much.

HANUMAN: Wise friend, I beg to differ –

LAKSHMAN: Good man, you have spent too much time
                                        among them.

HANUMAN: Quite right! I shall not mention them again.

LAKSHMAN: How could a monkey help us find our treasure?
  They are just beasts, that scream at one another,
  Fighting one moment, fast asleep the next –
  Moody and shallow!

HANUMAN: If you look at antbears.

LAKSHMAN: I beg your pardon?

HANUMAN: If you look at antbears –
  Even more inconsistent than the creatures
  That you just mentioned –

LAKSHMAN: What? Not them again?
  For God's sake let us talk about religion!

HANUMAN: Oh yes!

RAMA: I want to hear about these monkeys –
  This man of God is passionate about them –
  Men sparkle when they talk about their passions,
  They are divine.

HANUMAN: Believe me, sir, my passion
  Is God alone, and every word of scripture.
  Oh get me on the subject of religion!

RAMA: Go on then.

HANUMAN: God is –

LAKSHMAN: Rather like a monkey?

HANUMAN: Not quite!

RAMA: My friend, he is, by your description:
  You say that they are good at finding things –
  Well so is God – and good at doing nothing –
  Well God does nothing –

LAKSHMAN: Does he thrust his bum
  Into the air and scream like antbears mating?

HANUMAN: No he does not!

RAMA: But monkeys, I assume,
  Judging by how this man believes in them,
  Are loyal, brave, persistent, sharp-eyed, cunning –

LAKSHMAN: They are his passion.

RAMA: Shall I tell you mine?

HANUMAN nods.

It is my wife that we are looking for.
Her absence caused his tears. The demon King
Ravana took her, and he hides her nowhere.
She is my passion. And we two alone
Could search the world till we were old, for Sita –
That is my passion.

HANUMAN: We will look for her!

LAKSHMAN: Who will? The Brahmins?

RAMA: Thank you for your offer!

HANUMAN: Monkeys! Sugriva! Nila! Quick!

He leaps up and down in excitement and his cloak falls off, revealing that he is a monkey.

RAMA: What is your name?

HANUMAN: My name is Hanuman.
Forgive me for pretending! I was not a good Brahmin!

RAMA: You will grow great. And you will be my friend.
My name is Rama.

HANUMAN: On this jungle mountain,
Sugriva, brother of the tyrant Bali,
King of the monkeys, lives in dreadful exile
From our great city, beautiful Kishkindha!

RAMA: I am an exile.

HANUMAN: And Bali stole Sugriva's wife!

RAMA: Poor monkey.

HANUMAN: But in these trees around us, creeping closer,
Are thousands of his frightened followers,
And we will help you find your wife, Lord Rama!

RAMA: Brother of Bali, step into the open,
I am the man whose bow cuts down the demons.
I am Lord Rama. Let me see Sugriva!

Let us commend ourselves to one another,
And strike a deal. If I defeat your brother,
And set you in his place, will you, thereafter,
Employ your armies in the search for Sita?
My wife for your wife – and a crown and kingdom!

HANUMAN: Step out, Sugriva!

Enter JAMBAVAN. RAMA embraces him, slightly confused by the fact that he is a bear.

JAMBAVAN: I am not Sugriva. He won't come. I am Jambavan, King of the Bears.

RAMA: Welcome, Jambavan!

LAKSHMAN: Sugriva, quick, your destiny is waiting!

SUGRIVA: *(Off.)* Hanuman, have you got your eye on them?

HANUMAN: Of course, my Lord.

SUGRIVA: *(Off.)* Right, here I come!

RAMA: Why is he waiting?

JAMBAVAN: He's very frightened.

RAMA: Brother unjustly punished, see my bow
Laid on the ground – oh come into my arms!

Enter NILA. RAMA embraces him.

NILA: He is just coming. I am Nila.

RAMA: Welcome, Nila.

NILA: It's safe, Sugriva!

Enter SUGRIVA and others. RAMA embraces him.

RAMA: Take courage from my love!

SUGRIVA: Well you haven't killed us yet!

RAMA: You have good reason to be frightened.

SUGRIVA: I heard your offer. The first kind word I've heard in years! Well, this is a good day! God, you are warm! Hug me again. Rama! This is my curse – my bright blue arse, so beautiful it drives all other males insanc with jealousy. When I was born, my mother took one look at me and burst into

29

tears, crying – He is too beautiful to live! And if anything my beauty has grown since then. No wonder bad luck bursts out of the ground I tread on! But now my stars have changed their meaning!

RAMA: Your wife has been taken.

SUGRIVA: Your wife has been taken.

RAMA: You are an exile.

SUGRIVA: You are an exile.

RAMA: Oh my friend!

SUGRIVA: Oh my friend!

They embrace.

RAMA: I will be your protector, from humans, from elephants, from earthquakes and from fire! Creatures! It was a sad day when you were forced to flee from your city! I will lead you back today! I will sweep aside the tyrant, you will sleep under rooves again, see your wives, dream sweet dreams! I will give you back your courage!

HANUMAN: And we will give you back your wife!

Exeunt shouting and whooping. Sounds of battle off.

SCENE 9

Re-enter victorious all but RAMA and LAKSHMAN.

SUGRIVA: *(Sings.)* In the battle of this world
    I was running for my life,
    Out of my home city hurled
    By the one who took my wife!

MONKEYS: We were with you all the time.

SUGRIVA: Then at last I turned and roared,
    Gripped my courage in my fist,
    Like a hawk my spirit soared,
    Through my teeth my fury hissed!

MONKEYS: Down your legs you fiercely pissed!

SUGRIVA: And I seized my brother's head

And I ripped it from his shoulders;
Now the vultures are well-fed
On his bones among the boulders.

MONKEYS: Rama shot him from behind
When he was about to snap you,
You were flapping like a salmon,
You were screaming like a demon!

SUGRIVA: Beauty, victory and grace
Are all shining in my face –
I will credit any story,
Offer anyone the glory!

MONKEYS: Then you must give thanks to him!

TARA enters dancing and goes to SUGRIVA.

Rain starts.

JAMBAVAN: The rains!

SUGRIVA: We cannot look for Sita! This will delay us for three months!

HANUMAN: I will tell Rama!

SUGRIVA: Where is he?

HANUMAN: In a cave on the mountain – while he is an exile he cannot enter any building!

SUGRIVA: Say that we will meet him at the first glimpse of spring!

HANUMAN: I will tell him!

Exeunt.

SCENE 10

A cave on the mountain. RAMA and LAKSHMAN, watching the rains. Suddenly they stop. Silence descends.

LAKSHMAN: Where are the monkeys then? They should be here! At the end of the rains – they swore!

RAMA: Run to them, Lakshman! Tell them to set out – and give this ring to Hanuman!

Exeunt.

SCENE 11

Kishkhinda, the monkey city, SUGRIVA's throneroom. Enter MONKEYS, including TARA and MONKEY WOMEN, and JAMBAVAN and his wife. All are drunk except HANUMAN.

SUGRIVA: More beer! More beer! Till now we've only been sipping, now we must dive in, tip whole crates down, see what happens. I know! Let's play blind man's wife!

NILA: We haven't got any blind men!

SUGRIVA: This game was brought to us by trained monkeys, who escaped.

JAMBAVAN: Still I think we should call it blind monkey's wife!

SUGRIVA: You are a bear! Keep out of this! It's complex enough as it is, we're not going to play a game called blind monkey's or bear's or antbear's wife – the game has a name, and it's a good one.

NILA: Let's play pissed animals arguing!

SUGRIVA: We are playing blind man's wife! I am the King!

NILA: The king is drunk! The drunk is king!

HANUMAN: *(Aside.)* The rain stopped a week ago.
Monkeys have you forgotten your promise? Luckily for my king I have summoned our armies.

NILA: Your majesty – be the first blind man!

JAMBAVAN: No – me, me!

NILA: Let's all be blindfolded.

SUGRIVA: No! The husband wears the blindfold. And the women run round and round him. You must put on each other's voices and perfumes – confuse the husband! And if he chooses the wrong wife – she's his forever.

TARA: I don't want to lose you, husband!

HANUMAN: This will end in murder!

JAMBAVAN: Let me go first!

SUGRIVA: You are a bear! How many times do I have to explain that? You wife is also a bear – even more so you might say – how could you possibly mistake her for a monkey?

NILA: He's after something slim and bouncy!

JAMBAVAN: No I'm not!

SUGRIVA: The object of the game is to prove your love by finding your wife!

TARA: Let Jambavan be the first blind man!

SUGRIVA: Because you do not want to lose me?

JAMBAVAN is blindfolded.

HANUMAN: Your Majesty, I notice that the rains have ended.

SUGRIVA: What comes next? Winter? Spring?

HANUMAN: My King, you made a promise –

JAMBAVAN blunders about while the MONKEY and BEAR WOMEN run in circles around him.

NILA: Now monkey ladies – growl!

JAMBAVAN grabs TARA.

HANUMAN: Oh my God!

SUGRIVA: Take off his blindfold! So – you think my wife is a bear? Is that what you are saying?

JAMBAVAN: I couldn't see!

SUGRIVA: Take her! And I hope you like her!

JAMBAVAN: My King, I tripped! Take her back!

SUGRIVA: Shall I break my own rules? She is yours! God bless the pair of you, I hope you will be very happy and I never want to see either of you again!

JAMBAVAN: I don't want her!

SUGRIVA: Isn't she good enough for you?

HANUMAN: My friends!

They fight and HANUMAN tries to intervene. Everyone piles in.

LAKSHMAN: *(Off.)* Sugriva!

JAMBAVAN: Hello?

HANUMAN: It's Lakshman, furious, in the courtyard!

NILA: Ding dong!

HANUMAN: The rains have ended!

SUGRIVA: Before they had even begun!

HANUMAN: Your Majesty, you made a promise to meet God at a
cave when the rains ended, to help him look for his wife.

SUGRIVA: God – Majesty – cave –

HANUMAN: You have missed the meeting and now God's
brother is here, in fury!

Enter LAKSHMAN.

LAKSHMAN: Pitiful creatures! Worse than pigs or donkeys!
How could we think that our supreme adventure
Could be entrusted to the likes of monkeys?

SUGRIVA: Ah Lakshman!

LAKSHMAN: Do you remember what you swore to Rama?

HANUMAN: King, I have divided your forces into four legions
ready to set out in all directions.

SUGRIVA: You superior person.

LAKSHMAN: How your delay has made my brother suffer!

SUGRIVA: We will find her! We will find her!

LAKSHMAN: How could you leave him weeping in the jungle –

SUGRIVA: Hanuman, tell them: you to the west, you to the east,
you to the north, and you, Hanuman, lead the search to the
south as far as the great sea.

LAKSHMAN: How do you know they will not simply wander,
Following falling fruit until they die?

SUGRIVA: We will not disappoint you, Lakshman! Listen to the
law! Any monkey not returning within one month, unless he
brings news of Sita, will be killed, killed, killed! *(To JAMBAVAN.)*
And you – never come near me again!

JAMBAVAN: Too strict!

SUGRIVA: Not strict enough! If I could do worse than kill you I
    would! Malingerers! How long have you been searching and
    you still bring me nothing, nothing!

HANUMAN: We haven't started yet.

SUGRIVA: Why not?

LAKSHMAN: Hanuman, take this ring from Rama's finger,
    If you find Sita, this will prove your story,
    Which she may doubt, that you were sent by Rama.

HANUMAN: It is as bright as my desire to find her!

NILA: It is as round as going round in circles.

    Exeunt HANUMAN, NILA, JAMBAVAN, others.

LAKSHMAN: My rage is wider than the sky, Sugriva!

SUGRIVA: Can I offer you a glass of anything?

    Exeunt, LAKSHMAN harassing SUGRIVA.

SCENE 12

*Beside the southern ocean. Enter HANUMAN, JAMBAVAN, NILA, and others
in great dejection.*

HANUMAN: Keep going!

JAMBUVAN: Keep going!

NILA: What's the point?

JAMBAVAN: No turning back!

NILA: How could he do this to us? Are we his enemies?

JAMBAVAN: The King will relent! Look – we entered a mountain
    looking for Sita – we were in there for two days, no more, and
    when we came out, six weeks had passed!

NILA: The King's decree states that anyone not returning within
    four weeks, unless they bring news of Sita, will die –

JAMBAVAN: But time stopped!

NILA: I used to say that when I was late for school.

JAMBAVAN: But this time it's true!

NILA: Then I'd say that.

Oh what's this? My feet are wet!

JAMBAVAN: The sea!

HANUMAN: The sea!

NILA: I'm up to my knees.

JAMBAVAN: This is the end. We have searched the world. There is nothing beyond this point – just water.

HANUMAN: Rama will save us!

NILA: I know what to do! Listen to me! I think we should sit down here by the sea, about twelve yards apart from one another, and wait to die.

JAMBAVAN: I haven't got time.

NILA: You must make time. Death's important.

JAMBAVAN: Hanuman will save us.

NILA: You're special, aren't you, Hanuman?

Enter SAMPATI.

JAMBAVAN: Look! An eagle with no feathers!

HANUMAN: A sign!

NILA: Not a very hopeful sign.

SAMPATI: Welcome! I have been waiting by this ocean
For years. A prophecy foretold your coming.

HANUMAN: What did it say we would do?

NILA: Drown.

SAMPATI: Ask me where Sita is.

HANUMAN: Where is she?

SAMPATI: Sleeping
Under the peak one dawn, a sharp cry woke me
And I looked up and saw the demon King,
Ravana, flying to the south, a woman
Pressed to his breast and crying like a curlew.

HANUMAN: Where did he take her?

SAMPATI: To his capital,
    Lanka, two hundred miles across the water.

JAMBAVAN: What do you mean? There's nothing out there.

SAMPATI: It is a city on an island. There,
    Hawk-like, he stooped, and I could see no more.

JAMBAVAN: Eagle! The feathers you lost are in your head!
    Don't you know that this saltness is infinite?

SAMPATI: Infinite to a monkey or a bear,
    Not to an eagle. I have seen beyond it.

JAMBAVAN is about to complain. SAMPATI silences him.

I shall not argue! I have told you plainly
Where Sita is. Proceed across the sea
If you think you can do it! Now great heaven,
That spoke through me, is putting back my feathers!
I have performed my penance to the letter!

Exit.

JAMBAVAN: Hug me, monkeys! Victory! Victory!

NILA: Two hundred miles across the water. How far can you
    jump?

HANUMAN: For Sita I could jump – a hundred and fifty miles.

NILA: So close!

JAMBAVAN: You can do better than that!

HANUMAN: Can I?

JAMBAVAN: Ah Hanuman, Hanuman! Have you never heard
    the hints, never noticed us whispering about you behind your
    back? No! Your mind's on higher things!

NILA: When the wind moans like a mad old woman on a
    Monday morning, have you never felt, Hanuman, that you
    know what it's saying?

HANUMAN: No!

JAMBAVAN: Confess! When the breeze has tickled your tail at the
    top of a tree on a summer evening, have you never wondered
    why it thought it had the right to do that?

HANUMAN: No.

NILA: Think! When the big storm bangs its head against the mountain and pines go down in rows and the river blows backwards, have you never thought, I know how it feels – ?

HANUMAN: Not me.

JAMBAVAN: You have! You have! You must have done! Even I have felt these things and I am not the son of the wind!

HANMAN: What do you mean?

JAMBAVAN: Ask yourself what you are!

NILA: Hanuman, you are the son of the wind.

HANUMAN: The wind?

JAMBAVAN: Your mother, walking on the peak of a mountain on a still day, suddenly felt these breezy hands feeling her all over – and she thought there must be a storm coming, as the wind increased its excitement – everywhere else was still but round her there was a small tornado – then these invisible lips started pressing her fur – that was all she was wearing – oh she was a lovely monkey – then the wind gripped her, loved her everywhere at once, and swept her up into a cloud that boomed and crackled – and so you began.

HANUMAN: It's true – how can I tell you –

NILA: Look, we were only joking!

JAMBAVAN: No we were not! Don't listen to him!

HANUMAN: Why didn't you tell me this before?

JAMBAVAN: We were waiting for this moment! The gods told us to keep this a secret – they said you must not be told who you are until the moment when God himself needs your power. I've longed to tell you –

NILA: This'll change him.

HANUMAN: Is it true, my friends, not just the bear's blather?

NILE: You know I'd deny it if I could – I liked you quiet – but now, God help us!

JAMBAVAN: And the gods were right. You're not proud!

Maybe too much the opposite. But your power's still there!

HANUMAN: And I will leap across the sea to Sita!
    I am already there! I think I see her!
    Rama has found me! He has set me free,
    I can do all things by his love for me!

NILA: Look out! Hanuman's expanding!

JAMBAVAN: Out of the way!

HANUMAN: I am immense!

JAMBAVAN: Get down!

NILA: He leaps!

HANUMAN: I am the breath of Rama!

Exit HANUMAN.

JAMBAVAN: The mountain's collapsed!

NILA: Look at that –

They climb on top of each other trying to glimpse HANUMAN as he disappears.

JAMBAVAN: Taller than a million chimneys!

NILA: And the smoke coming out of them!

Exeunt.

SCENE 13

LANKA, in the Ashoka grove. Enter DEMON WOMEN and SITA.

FIRST DEMONESS: Where is Rama all this time?

SECOND DEMONESS: Ten months his wife has withered in this place.

FIRST DEMONESS: And still the man is nowhere to be seen!

SECOND DEMONESS: Is he afraid of demons?

FIRST DEMONESS: He's destroyed
    Ten thousand of them in one afternoon.

SECOND DEMONESS: Where is he then? In heaven?
                                         On the moon?

FIRST DEMONESS: Under the ground?

SECOND DEMONESS: Is Rama dead, you mean?

FIRST DEMONESS: Impossible! His life has just begun!

SECOND DEMONESS: Free of his wife!

FIRST DEMONESS: They say that when this man,
  Banished for nothing, had to leave his home,
  He pleaded with his wife to stay behind.

SECOND DEMONESS: He did not want her in the forest then?

FIRST DEMONESS: With all the female spirits of the trees
  For entertainment?

SECOND DEMONESS: But he loves his princess!

FIRST DEMONESS: Only because his guru told him to.

SECOND DEMONESS: Her father is a wealthy King, it's true.

FIRST DEMONESS: The vows of Princes are political.

SECOND DEMONESS: They love like whores, for gold and silver.

FIRST DEMONESS: And look for passion and true sighs

  Out of the corners of their eyes.

SECOND DEMONESS: But Rama is a god?

FIRST DEMONESS: What woman
  On earth could satisfy him then?
  He needs a million every day,
  A dancing naked milky way!

SECOND DEMONESS: But I believe that he is just a man.

FIRST DEMONESS: The same applies. What gods already have,
  Man needs. The only difference is the means,
  Which man is lacking. So he goes insane!

SECOND DEMONESS: My dear, I think Lord Rama loves
  this woman,
  It's just your twisted mind.

FIRST DEMONESS: Where is he then?

SECOND DEMONESS: He loves her like the sun!

FIRST DEMONESS: Long winter then!

Exeunt. RAVANA approaches, carried in an open palanquin. He addresses SITA.

RAVANA: Is Rama God? Then what is God? Not perfect,
Since he created me, the great wrongdoer!
So his own imperfection will destroy him!
But what is god? A wish requiring proof.
I prove myself each moment of the day
By acting my desires as they occur.
You make me wait. And this has changed my nature.
I question what I am, and grow in stature,
By self-reflection I am multiplied!
Speak to me, Sita! *(To DEMONS.)* You must offer her
All that I have! Unclasp my caskets to her!
(Aside to SOORPANAKHA.) Have you hurt her?

SOORPANAKHA: Not yet.

RAVANA: Have you terrified her?

SOORPANAKHA: We have tried!

RAVANA: Who are these little kings caged in your eyes, both the same, amber-flies. Me? Split by the bridge of your nose, cut off, screaming. I have seen you in my mirror. How did you get there?

SITA recites the name of RAMA. He addresses her again, less patiently.

I'll tell you a poem. Sun gets up, rises, rises – then starts to sink down. Not me! What I have inside gets higher, brighter, higher, brighter – no night ever!

SITA continues to recite the name of RAMA.

How long can you do that for? I prayed on a mountain till the wind stopped, world cried out, strangled, God came down, crying, crying, said 'Please stop, you are so still, world can't breathe, please move!' I would not.

God had to negotiate.
I will stare out the passing of your body
Into the dust, and love the little flowers
That peep between your bones to look for summer!

41

SITA recites. RAVANA finally explodes.

Humans are just mirrors – when a god walks by – ah! –
when a demon walks by – ah, terror! You will shatter, Sita!
Look – fire says, come, we will be one! Share with me! You
must fear! You must fear! What is flesh, but fear? Feed me!
Soorpanakha!

Enter SOORPANAKHA and DEMON WOMEN.

Words have done what words can.

*He signs for the women to attack SITA. SOORPANAKHA and the whores
torture her.*

Want me as I want you, or one more month from now, you
end, and this magnificent invention of God, I, like an angry
child in a cot, will break and throw back in his face!

Exit.

SOORPANAKHA: And every hour we will return with torture.
When the gong sounds, expect our visit, Sita!

Exeunt all but SITA. Enter HANUMAN flying.

HANUMAN: I see the thousand-towered tree-filled city.
Oh what a roof for evil, what a veil
Of greenery for cruelty! I glide
Through a vast arch into a marble hall
So white the floor and ceiling disappear –
Look – on the walls this mark – the mace and goad,
And painted lotuses and swastikas,
Symbol of purity – what hypocrisy!
This is the city of a cultured people.
Generous, gracious, elegant and evil.
But where is Sita, diamond in the dunghill!
A window, like a picture framed in gold –
Oh God! The wives of Ravana, all strewn
In heaps like clothes flung off for love, red wine
Staining their lips that mouth their husband's name
As they cry out, believing in their dream
That he is with them! And they clutch each other!
I have to get away from here! I'm falling

Into a garden! Too late! Help, crash-landing!

He crashes into the ground in the Ashoka grove where SITA is lying, and jumps into a tree.

I seek a woman. Could this be the one?

He touches her.

SITA: Get off me, demon.

HANUMAN: I am Hanuman!

SITA: A monkey.

HANUMAN: Do you recognise this ring?

He shows her RAMA's ring.

SITA: You are a demon! This is an illusion!

HANUMAN: Oh Rama, you should not have sent me here!
    How can I prove you sent me? Rama, Rama!
    I should have stayed beside you where the air
    Is bright with trust – what am I doing here?

SITA is convinced by HANUMAN's passion.

SITA: Rama is here!

HANUMAN: I think you must be Sita.

SITA: Rama is here!

HANUMAN: Not Rama - just his ring.

SITA: Rama is here!

HANUMAN: You mean his ring is him?

SITA: For ten dead months I have not heard his name.
    Now he is here with me, I there with him.

HANUMAN: Heavenly Mother, hear my story! Rama
    Became the ally of my King Sugriva,
    And they are ready with a monkey army
    To come for you as soon as you are found.

SITA: How did you get here?

HANUMAN: Leaped across the sea.
    And now I will leap back with him to you!

SITA: I can touch him only, no other being.

HANUMAN: How can you touch him if you cannot reach him,
 How can you reach him, over that wide ocean,
 If you do not touch me?

SITA: No, Hanuman!

HANUMAN: He is my father – so you are my mother!
 How can a mother fear to touch her child?

SITA: My child you must not argue with your mother!
 Ravana stole me, Rama must release me
 By open means, and not by robbery,
 However honest. He must come to me
 In person, in command of righteous armies!
 If we are ruled by what we want to do,
 Not by the strength of right, then we are nothing;
 People would laugh forever at the story
 Of how a monkey did the work for Rama,
 And pilfered Sita from her pilferer!

HANUMAN: Forgive me – it was never my intention
 To stain his name – it is my only honour.

SITA: Do not go just yet – speak to me about him!

HANUMAN: I want to leave so that I can return!

SITA: Oh tell my Lord that if he does not come
 Within one month, I will have vanished, tell him
 That I would love to see him one more time
 Before my soul escapes from this illusion.

HANUMAN: Nothing will stop me!

HANUMAN leaps about, beating his chest.

SITA: Down! You will be seen!

Enter DEMON WOMEN.

FIRST DEMONESS: Come to your mummy! Look!
          A bag of nutsies!

SECOND DEMONESS: And we will only cut your throat!

FIRST DEMONESS: Be quiet!

44

Monkey!

He breaks trees and whirls them about.

FIRST DEMONESS: Look out! He wants to kill us!

SECOND DEMONESS: Sound the alarm!

SECOND DEMONESS: Indrajit!

Enter INDRAJIT and DEMON SOLDIERS.

INDRAJIT: Soldiers of the guard, surround it!
Monster, who sent you?

HANUMAN: I will tell you nothing
Till I am speaking to the thief your king!

INDRAJIT: Attack!

SOLDIERS attack from all sides. HANUMAN kills them, but INDRAJIT shoots an arrow that knocks HANUMAN down.

               This arrow has been blessed by Brahma,
No living creature can resist its power!

The SOLDIERS bind HANUMAN with chains and carry him off.

SCENE 14

RAVANA's throneroom. Enter DEMONS with HANUMAN.

RAVANA: Summoned for a monkey? Kill it by a ditch – kick it in!

HANUMAN: Would it be right to kill a messenger?

RAVANA: What is your message?

HANUMAN: Ravana, return Sita to Rama or his army of monkeys
will trample your city!

COUNCILLORS laugh.

Demons, beware, I am the first of millions!

RAVANA: And we will catch them too. So you are a messenger –
we will send a message with you back to your master. Bind his
tail in pitch-soaked rags. Set them alight. March him through
the streets, proclaiming his message and that this is our
answer. Then let him hop smoking back to Rama!

As he says this, HANUMAN's tail is bound and lit and he exits with SOLDIERS.

Rama! Send no more freaks, no fighting monkeys, or speaking fish, come yourself, we will teach you terror, we are more monstrous than your monsters!

COUNCILLORS laugh. Flickering of flames behind them. Outcry. Enter SOLDIER.

SOLDIER: Run! Run!

RAVANA: From what?

SOLDIER: The beast shrank in its chains and slipped out of them! It leapt up a house and ran off across the rooves and where he had been we saw tiny sickles of flame, that jumped up, each one a destroying monkey, all joining – whole buildings are nothing but fire, bright flesh on black bones, that crash like skies collapsing!

RAVANA: *(To COUNCILLORS.)* Summon your forces to fight the fire-army!

Exeunt all but RAVANA.

(Cries out.) The city is myself – this fire is Sita!

Enter VIBISHANA.

VIBISHANA: You must confess, the argument of fire
    Destroys your case for keeping Sita's brother!

RAVANA: You do not know how much I love her.

VIBISHANA: Demons! The sin our king committed
    Has turned the elements against us!
    Lanka will vanish in a flash;
    Goodness and gladness go together,
    Evil brings misery and disaster!
    Sita is death! We must return her!

RAVANA: Liar!

He attacks VIBISHANA and wounds him but VIBISHANA escapes.

VIBISHANA: Because you will not listen you are nothing!
        I will escape across the sea to Rama!

Exit.

RAVANA: Can he not understand that war with Rama
    Is what the demons have desired forever?

Exit.

SCENE 15

Kishkindha. Enter MONKEYS, RAMA, BEARS.

HANUMAN: I acted like a monkey! When they lit me,
    I got excited and burned down the city!
    Forgive me, Lord, I will improve, I swear!
    I have seen Sita! By your love for me
    She has been found – and I will lead you to her!

NILA: How will we cross the sea?

SUGRIVA: Trust lord Rama.

NILA: Yes but what happens when we get to the sea?
    Hanuman has changed but nothing's happened to me!
    I want to be blessed!

RAMA: Nila, what is it that you want me to do for you?

NILA: I would like to fly through the air!

RAMA: Hasn't that been done already?

NILA: I want to walk through fire!

RAMA: Why not go round?

NILA: I want to do something! Lift mountains!

RAMA: Oh leave the poor things where they are!

NILA: Well you choose then, Rama, whoever you are!
    If you can make Hanuman jump over oceans –

RAMA: That's his speciality.

NILA: But he couldn't do it before he met you! Don't try to
    outsmart me. Am I nothing or am I something? If I am
    something, make me that thing!

RAMA: I will if you stop complaining.

NILA: When will that be?

RAMA: Who knows?

NILA: This is ridiculous!

RAMA: To the south, whoever has something to find!

Exeunt, leaping and shouting.

SCENE 16

By the sea. RAMA and LAKSHMAN, RAMA sings to the ocean.

RAMA: Beautiful ocean, wide as night,
Crowning joy of human sight,
Lovely as a field of dew,
Part, and let my army through!

LAKSHMAN: It will not shift!

RAMA: You see our monkey army,
Millions, a ribbon pasted to the coastline,
For mile and miles – they crowd into the sea,
Or stand bewildered; listen to the murmur
Of puzzled voices – and I brought them here!

Enter MONKEYS and JAMBAVAN and VIBISHANA.

SUGRIVA: We caught this demon creeping out of the cloud cover.
We would have torn him to pieces, but he cried out for Rama.
So we've brought him to you. Watch him!

RAVANA: What is your name?

VIBISHANA: Vibishana. I surrender
To you, Lord Rama.

HANUMAN: Then he is the brother
Of Ravana!

RAMA: But from now on – my brother!

NILA: A demon!

JAMBAVAN: We trust your judgement.

HANUMAN: We bow to it!

NILA: Look at the sea now! Answer me! How can we march
across that?

LAKSHMAN: Go swimming, monkey!

He grabs NILA angrily as if to throw him into the sea.

RAMA: What shall we do? How shall we cross the sea?

VIBISHANA: Clearly the sea is sleeping. We must wake him.

RAMA: Thank you! Varuna, you have kept me waiting!

Now I will make you desert, rebel sea!

He is about to shoot an arrow. VARUNA speaks, off.

VARUNA: I am Varuna. Rama, I have come.

RAMA: Permit my army to pass through you, ocean.

VARUNA: You made me, God, and by a strict command
Gave me my nature, which is that of water.
I can be calm, but I cannot be land!
You must cut stones and carve them with your name,
And they will float. A causeway built from them
Will take your army to the walls of Lanka!

RAMA: Nila, you will be the one to place the stones on the water!

The MONKEYS start carving RAMA's name on rocks and passing them down a line to make a causeway. NILA stands at the end placing them on the water.

NILA: It floats! Bloody hell! A fluke! I'll try another one. It floats! I'm getting good at this. Hey, I'm a bridge-builder! Don't slack – keep them coming! Carve Rama on them – that's it – R – A – M – A – spell it right or it won't work – I don't want anything shoddy.

MONKEYS carve and pass rocks down the line, singing, 'sita ram ram ram, sita ram ram ram –'

HANUMAN: Each letter brings us closer to battle!

SUGRIVA: No need to hurry the work – take pride in what you're doing –

NILA: How many of them are there?

SUGRIVA: At least twice as many as us! And thy know no fear.

In fear they all start chanting twice as loud to RAMA and dance the building of the bridge.

SCENE 17

RAVANA's bedchamber. Enter RAVANA and MANDODARI.

RAVANA: They have surrounded the city. Monkeys like hills moving. They howl all night outside the gates. It is ourselves, come to feast on ourselves!

MANDODARI: My Lord –

RAVANA: Do you hear screaming? They have caught someone! Now fling him from claw to claw high up – you have seen what they did to my sister!

MANDODARI: That was Lord Rama and his brother.

RAVANA: So much the worse their hired murderers! Will tear me, toy with me, hang me from a hundred trees!

MANDODARI: Your death is coming! Listen to me, King!

RAVANA: I shall not speak.

MANDODARI: You shall not fight Lord Rama!
How can a candle's anger hurt the sun?
Rama is all things. You must not approach him
With burning anger but with warm devotion
Bow down, and like the earth draw strength from him,
Not death! Return the woman you have stolen!

RAVANA: I had a dream. I was the keeper of the door of heaven and a holy man cursed me because I would not let him in, that I should be born on earth as a demon but that when the Lord of All came down as a man and killed me, I would return!

MANDODARI: You see, my husband, you were meant for
heaven!
You will return – but must it be destruction
That lifts you up? There is another splendour,
Brighter than conquest – heavenly surrender!

RAVANA: Surrender? When I have the universe

Trapped in my palace, waiting to be mine?
She shall surrender, I shall not surrender!

MANDODARI: I love you and I do not wish to see you
Cut down, your beauty scattered like a forest
Smashed by a stormwind! Think about your dream!
Have you forgotten? Is your strength of mind
Obliterated utterly by Sita?
Sita is not for you, my love – remember!

RAVANA: You make me old – she makes me live forever,

And with that life I make the death of Rama!

Exit. Sound of war-conches and screaming. MANDODARI covers her ears.

SCENE 18

Outside Lanka. Enter SUGRIVA running from the fight, to RAMA.

SUGRIVA: Help me! Help me!

Enter JAMBAVAN.

JAMBAVAN: King – get back into the fight or we will all follow!

SUGRIVA: I hate you! Get away from me!

RAMA: King! Jump onto his back. That will make you brave!

SUGRIVA jumps onto JAMBAVAN's back.

SUGRIVA: My friend, forgive me!

JAMBAVAN: Charge!

They fight DEMONS. Exeunt and re-enter.

JAMBAVAN: Where is Indrajit, the King's son? I changed his face
with my claws. He fell back, spat blood, and disappeared!

VIBISHANA: He can become invisible! Beware!

SUGRIVA: He could be aiming at us now!

VIBISHANA: Get down!

LAKSHMAN: Stand up! Stand up! The victory is ours!
Do not be frightened by a figment!

LAKSHMAN is shot down.

RAMA: Lakshman!

HANUMAN: Surround Lord Rama! Shield him with yourselves!

INDRAJIT: *(Off.)* Where shall I shoot? Guts, eyes, arse, balls?
   Jump, monkeys!

   The MONKEYS dance around trying to protect themselves.

SUGRIVA: Escape! Escape!

HANUMAN: Stand firm around Lord Rama!

VIBISHANA: He cannot stay invisible for long!
   Do not be frightened! He will be retreating!
   He has retreated, I am certain.

RAMA: Lakshman!

VIBISHANA: Is Lakshman dead?

RAMA: My brother! Oh! My brother!

HANUMAN: My Lord!

JAMBAVAN: Lord Rama, Lakshman is not dead! This is paralysis.

VIBISHANA: Could he be alive after that arrow?

JAMBAVAN: I know the herbs that can cure him – they grow
   on the mountain of herbs far away back the other side of
   the ocean in the Himalayas, between the peaks of Rishabha
   and Kailasha – the ones I need are Sandhani, Mritsamjirani,
   Vishalyakarani, and Suvarakarani – Hanuman, could you
   leap that far?

HANUMAN: I am not wounded.

VIBISHANA: Could he be alive
   After that arrow?

JAMBAVAN: Monkey, leap and save him!

HANUMAN: I am already wider than the wind,
   I am already taller than the mountain!

JAMBAVAN: Stand back!

   Exeunt.

52

SCENE 19

LAKSHMAN's body. RAMA and all the others except HANUMAN.

RAMA: Midnight! Perhaps my servant Hanuman
 Has lost his way and plunged into the ocean
 At the far limit of his leap! And Lakshman
 Still hangs unhelped above his own destruction;
 Open your eyes! I have not looked at them
 Since yesterday! You have watched over me
 For such a long time, never even blinking;
 How can you close your eyes and let me be?
 You have abandoned your position, Lakshman!
 No other voice but yours on earth can tell me
 That you are well! This brother followed me,
 Although he did not have to, from our city;
 Leaving his parents and his wife for me,
 He suffered in the forest. He was like
 A rock above my head, he did not feel
 The sun, the rain; when food was hard to find,
 He gave whatever he could glean to me,
 And slept contented on the gound unfed;
 Look at this man! Observe the rich reward
 Of love and service! If I had foretold
 This end, he would have served me just the same,
 Because his nature was unquestioning.
 Lakshman, are you considering my needs?
 I need your eyes to open, do you know
 That for twelve hours you have not looked at me?

Enter HANUMAN carrying the entire mountain.

HANUMAN: I found the mountain, and it was bursting with herbs
 but they all looked the same. I almost turned inside out trying
 to work out what to do – jump back and ask again? Lakshman
 dying and the demons beating their drums! I thought, what
 can I do? What can I not do, given that the God of all things
 loves me! I bent down and tugged at the mountain – whose
 rock-roots for a moment stubbornly clung and then gave like
 the end of long constipation – the whole thing bounced out of
 the ground and came to rest in my hands. And I leapt –

The MONKEYS see HANUMAN. JAMBAVAN runs up and picks the herbs and gives them to LAKSHMAN, who rises. The MONKEYS go wild with excitement. Suddenly darkness descends.

VIBISHANA: Indrajit! He has put the sun out! Rama!
We must attack him in his sacred grove!
If he completes his incantations, nothing
In hell or heaven will prevail against him.

Exeunt.

SCENE 20

Enter INDRAJIT to his grove. He is in a place not reachable from the main stage, above and apart. He carries the body of a monkey he has just sacrificed.

INDRAJIT: Mother darkness, lake reflecting
Sky without light – consume their eyesight!

He clicks his fingers and the MONKEYS are plunged into darkness.

INDRAJIT: Light god man ape lizard fish slime nothing!
Monkeys grovel on the ground!

MONKEYS are flung sprawling to the ground.

INDRAJIT: Orca swiftness, tiger hunger,
Ocean anger, monkey terror!

MONKEYS are thrown into terror.

INDRAJIT: Fire in the head put out, pull down
Into claw and fang – confusion.

The MONKEYS start to fight one another. Exeunt.

SCENE 21

INDRAJIT's sacred grove. Enter INDRAJIT, in magician's cape and hat, to his torture instruments. He brings with him several MONKEY prisoners bound.

INDRAJIT: We have not simply stopped you praying,
We have eclipsed the fact of heaven!
Each murder and each massacre
Outdoes the one before in horror –
It is not bodies that we torture,

But the whole human mind, that screams
Into the void, how can our maker
Permit such things to happen?

*He activates the head-screw. MONKEY screams. INDRAJIT puts the next
MONKEY into the sawing-in-half machine.*

Now you! The story of your torture
Will be an everlasting nightmare!
This is our work – to drag down heaven
And in its place to set up terror!

*He saws the MONKEY in half. He places the sword-through-the-throat
device on the next MONKEY.*

And you! Be proud! The fate you suffer
Will turn good children into killers!

*He stabs the monkey through the throat. Exit MONKEY screaming. He
addresses the audience.*

Terror is the best teacher, instilling a tradition of hatred and
ignorance. So we unravel God's creation, whose foundations
are love and faith and wisdom. We will set up our own! Now
in the face of what we have done, parents have no answers to
the questions of their children! As a frightened child lets go of
a balloon, the world has let go – oh let go of heaven!

He goes to his shrine.

Their screaming has increased my power,
But I can lift it even higher
By even darker incantations.

He chants.

Sita in my father's bed,
Rama at the door, rejected.
Sita crying out for more,
As their sweat descends together.
All of heaven in the world
Cannot fight the fact of that,
Tiger on a tiger's back,
Dog on dog and rat on rat!

VIBISHANA: Indrajit!

INDRAJIT: Uncle! Are you here? The traitor
    Comes home! And it will make me shake with joy,
    To kill an older relative, to heal
    My flesh of this inherited disease!

LAKSHMAN: Not him – we have disturbed your ecstasies,
    And cut your power from its source.

INDRAJIT: Why are you fighting for my father's wife?

LAKSHMAN: Sita belongs to Rama!

INDRAJIT: Her desire
    Is to be free of Rama!

LAKSHMAN: You are lying!

INDRAJIT: Sita is in the arms of Ravana,
    They shunt and shudder in a shaking bed,
    While all around them monkeys scream at demons!
    I think new lovers should be left alone!

LAKSHMAN: I will reply by fighting.

INDRAJIT: But remember –
    Sita is in the arms of Ravana,
    And as we rush with spears at one another,
    His arms outflank her, and he pierces her
    With swift attacks into her very centre!

*LAKSHMAN goes to attack INDRAJIT. INDRAJIT with a gesture freezes
LAKSHMAN and VIBISHANA. LAKSHMAN is still able to chant the
name of RAMA. INDRAJIT ties LAKSHMAN to the turning-around board.*

INDRAJIT: Now by the power of my sword
    I will transform you into nothing!

*The turning-around board turns around and LAKSHMAN emerges.
INDRAJIT is tied up in his place. LAKSHMAN kills INDRAJIT.
VIBISHANA is immediately unfrozen, and runs to his nephew.*

INDRAJIT: Oh, Uncle!

VIBISHANA: Nephew, you are full of wounds.

INDRAJIT: They are illusions – you are in my power –
    Take care! Your heads are turning into flowers!

He dies.

VIBISHANA: He lived by lies and died believing them.

Exeunt. Enter RAMA to MONKEYS.

RAMA: You must not fear the darkness of the sky!
Monkeys, the sun and moon and stars will fail,
But when they darken, you must look within,
Where I shine brighter than a world of flame!
What do you fear, when you are seeds of me?
I am not I, I am the air you breathe,
And I am your best thought. Or you are Ravana?
This is your choice forever and forever –
We will destroy the evil we have seen,
But there will always be this choice for creatures,
Either or Rama or Ravana.
You must all rise as God or fall as demons,
There is no stasis, all is evolution,
But in the end, of all that has been scattered,
None will be lost, all will return to heaven.

SCENE 22

The grove. Enter MANDODARI, keening over the body of INDRAJIT. Enter RAVANA and SOORPANAKHA.

RAVANA: There is no other way.
My son lies here, the better warrior;
Our only hope is to remove the cause,
And it must be
That Sita is the centre of this order,
That when I kill her
The sun will burst and life will end and then,
I will begin the universe again.

MANDODARI: *(Aside.)* The time has come to turn against
my husband.
Ravana!

RAVANA: Queen! When I have murdered her,
You will be my one love, as once before!

MANDODARI: How can it be, my Lord, that you have fallen
    So low as to be forced to threaten murder
    Against the wife of Rama, when the man
    Himself is here, and ready to be conquered?
    Your army sinks because till now its leader,
    Beauty-besotted, has not fought beside it.
    But now the time has come to end confusion!

RAVANA: My Queen! Have you remembered who I am?

MANDODARI: Till now I have advised against this war,
    But now I have remembered how my husband
    Marched against death, besieged the gods in heaven!
    And I have seen that Rama is a man!
    Oh how could I have doubted him I love!

RAVANA: It will be greater and it will be sweeter
    To conquer Rama than to murder Sita!

    RAVANA builds himself up for battle. MANDODARI exits in tears. RAVANA
    is armed and to the sound of trumpets goes out to the fight.

SCENE 23

The Ashoka grove. Enter MANDODARI to SITA.

MANDODARI: My Queen!

SITA: My friend! You must not speak to me!

MANDODARI: The end is near. My husband has been fighting
    Your husband on the ground and in the air
    For eighteen days! The demon King called down
    A rain of sand and filled the battlefield
    With imps and goblins, but Lord Rama crushed them,
    And with his crescent arrows
    Cut off my husband's heads, but like desire
    They grow back quickly! There has never been
    A fight like this on earth!

SITA: It will not end!

MANDODARI: It it because your face is in his heart;
    It is your face that feeds them both with power,
    But Rama's heart is a sustaining heaven,

Ravana's an intolerable oven,
In which your face already chars and changes;
And when it fades, your husband will defeat him.
I tried to stop this, but the time has come
Simply to wish for Rama's victory
To free my husband from himself, the prison
That he builds up with every breath of freedom.

Exit.

SCENE 24

Outside the city. Enter RAMA and VIBISHANA.

VIBISHANA: Lord, when his necks are cut through one by one,
The stumps grow back new heads as quick as dying;
Now you must shoot sufficient to remove
Ten heads at once, and all his legs and arms –
And this – the sac he hides beneath his navel,
Full of the sap of immortality;
He cannot die if that is not destroyed.

RAMA: My arrows must drive Sita from his mind!

Enter RAVANA.

RAVANA: How dare you come across the sea to take away my
love, she who has taken away my nights, replaced my days
with her eyes, she whose sweet breathing brings to an end
time, death, grief, and all your other hired killers! You are not
worthy of her! She is my infinite power!

RAMA shoots off heads.

Grow back, my heads, do not desert me – hurry!
Restore me to the memory of my glory!

His heads return.

Each arrow that you shoot uplifts my glory
Into the human mind which will remember
Ravana, world lord, conqueror of Rama!

He attacks and RAMA shoots off some heads again, that rally.

VIBISHANA: *(To RAMA.)* She is no longer in his heart! Now kill him!

RAVANA: Rama! Rama! Rama! I adore you with rage, I worship you with death, I sacrifice you to yourself, God, Vishnu, Rama!

RAMA: Truth will kill you! I have killed all your sons, all your armies have been crushed by my monkeys, there is nothing left but you now, Ravana! My fourteen years of exile end today. That is the only reason why I have let this fight go on so long.

RAMA loads his bow with thirty-one arrows and shoots as RAVANA rushes at him. RAVANA's heads are all shot away and he collapses, all the heads still crying 'Rama! Rama! Rama!' RAMA rushes over to the body.

RAVANA's spirit emerges from his body.

RAMA: By hate you were devoted to my name;
Now you rush upwards in a rage of flame;
Great spirit, this is all my victory,
That I am in your heart and you are free!

Exit spirit. Enter MONKEYS, LAKSHMAN, JAMBAVAN.

LAKSHMAN: Total surrender. They have all turned into children. One monkey leads a thousand of them by the hand.

HANUMAN: Sita is coming.

NILA: What will she look like? They say Ravana tortured her.

JAMBAVAN: But he did not force himself upon her.

NILA: Can you still believe that? I pray it is true!

Enter SITA. She gets down from the palanquin and walks towards RAMA.

RAMA puts out his hand. SITA comes to a stop a little way from RAMA and they look at each other.

RAMA: *(To others.)* She has been living with another man.
I cannot take her back.

NILA: Who says he touched her?

RAMA: It has been said, and it will be believed
By some – by those who would believe it even

If it had not been said. When I am King,
I will control my people by example,
And not by force, and so my reputation
Must be unstained. I cannot take a woman
Another man is rumoured to have taken.

NILA: I should have died!

SITA: Heap up a pyre for me!

RAMA: Do what she says!

SUGRIVA: Destroy our victory?

RAMA: If you believe her, heap up wood for her.

NILA: We will not do it! You are wrong, Rama!

JAMBAVAN: We will not do it! Carry Sita away from here!

HANUMAN: I will not do it!

RAMA: Shrinking, Hanuman?

SITA: Lakshman, good man, have you forgiven me?

LAKSHMAN: I fought for you! Have you forgiven me
   For leaving you?

SITA: Dear brother, set me free
   From this dishonour – build a pyre for me.
   Monkeys! Why put me back into a prison
   Worse than the one you fought to free me from?
   Your final battle is to build my pyre,
   To burn the rumour that would be my warden.
   If the fire burns me, I was false to Rama,
   If its heat spares me, nothing stains my honour!

JAMBAVAN: I won't leave her standing there dishonoured!
   If the fire burns her, I'll join her in there!

NILA: So will I – I won't believe the fire!

SUGRIVA: Monkeys – do what she says! We are her servants –
   build her pyre!

SITA: Thank you, new friends. I hope to know you more.

LAKSHMAN: Forgive me!

SITA: If you look me in the eyes!
There, you have done it, we are friends. Thank heaven!

The pyre is built.

Husband and God, I ask you for your prayers,
To make us one, as we have been before.

She enters the fire. It does not burn her. She emerges unscathed.

Enter BHARATHA.

BHARATHA: Rama! Return, the fourteen years are over!

RAMA: You have done well to find me, Bharatha!
When we have crowned Vibishana King of Lanka,
We will set out together for Ayodhya.
Now we are one, my love, and so our drama
Is at an end. What have we done, you own.

Exeunt.

The End.

WWW.OBERONBOOKS.COM

Follow us on www.twitter.com/@oberonbooks
& www.facebook.com/OberonBooksLondon